G000128089

Good Business

ETHICS AT WORK

Advices and queries
on personal standards
of conduct at work

Contents

3 Introduction
6 Quaker Testimonies
10 Conduct of Business
18 Money Matters
24 Working with People
31 The Community
34 Unethical Business Practices
37 Balancing Vision with Practice
42 Quaker Methods for Decision Making
44 Useful Contacts
46 List of Subjects
48 The Quakers and Business Group

Published by
The Quakers and Business Group
Quaker Meeting House
58 Alexandra Grove
London NI2 8HG
UK

ISBN 0-9539706-0-4

Designed by
Benjamin Rowntree Design

Printed by
Warwick Printing Company Limited
Theatre Street
Warwick CV34 4DR
UK

Good Business: Ethics at Work

Introduction

William Penn, an early Quaker, said "True godliness don't *(sic)* turn men out of the world but enables them to live better in it and excites their endeavours to mend it...". Quakers believe that, as we grow in awareness of God's will for our lives, we begin to translate our experience of the holy into active life. Hence, we have always emphasised integrity in personal conduct and service in the betterment of the world and its people as an integral part of our spiritual life. Many Quaker businesses have been recognised as forerunners in fair trading, good business practice and care for employees.

For many years Quakers have used a booklet entitled *Advices and Queries* as a challenge and inspiration in their personal lives. Those advices and queries are not rules or requirements; rather they represent ideals to aspire to and standards of excellence to guide us in our personal and corporate conduct. It is in this spirit that we offer these advices and queries for people in business.

This book is addressed to anyone working in any kind of enterprise who is concerned with ethics in business. It has been published by a group of Quakers, all of whom have worked, or are working, in a variety of businesses run with the intention of making a profit. We believe that we should live our lives in accordance with our beliefs. We try to do so, and we believe our work in business and our spiritual lives to be compatible.

Not everyone shares our view. Today many people, Quakers and others, are so dismayed at the unethical business practices they see around them that they have come to believe that business itself is unethical.

Some question whether the world of business is compatible with our testimonies on social justice, equality, peace and the environment. Others wonder whether a system which implies varying rewards for effort is consistent with our most fundamental belief in respecting that of God in everyone. We respect their concerns. We respect the similar concerns of those in other Christian denominations and the concerns of other faiths. Yet we remain sure of our conviction.

The world of work is an imperfect one. We know as authors that we have not lived up to all the advice offered, and could not honestly say we could answer every query in this book in the affirmative. We recognise that this is part of being human. We recognise that some business activities are inappropriate. We acknowledge that there can be an "unacceptable face of capitalism". Yet we are called to live in the world. We believe that through the interaction of our faith and our ability in business we can help provide those resources we all need to live our lives.

These advices and queries cannot cover every business circumstance but our faith is an experimental one – an adventurous one. These offerings are our interpretations of the world of work as we see it, and the questions we might ask of ourselves. We offer them in that spirit so that they might assist others when faced with a problem requiring resolution. Resolving problems is the art of management. Remember the ends for your action, as well as the means. If that objective is important and consistent with your faith then the action will be worthwhile, and appropriate means must be found. If it is not, then restraint or further consideration is required.

This, we believe, is faith in action in the workplace, whether that be the home, office, shop, field or factory, for wherever people are at work, there is that of God within them.

The principal authors are members of The Quakers and Business Group, but we would like to acknowledge the many contributions and support which have come from the conference on Business and Ethics run by Woodbrooke Quaker Study Centre, Birmingham, UK, in June 2000, and many other people in the UK and the USA. Likewise, we have in some instances drawn upon *Quaker Faith & Practice*, published by The Yearly Meeting of the Religious Society of Friends (Quakers) in Britain. References to the corresponding paragraph numbers in *Quaker Faith & Practice* are indicated in parenthesis. (.. ..)

Quaker Testimonies

There are four basic testimonies which have sprung from our faith and into which we have been guided over the years. They are not imposed or required of Friends, but are part of our distinctive witness. We start with these four fundamental testimonies, which we believe apply to all our lives, and interpret them in a business context.

1. Honesty and integrity

Advice
: The most important word to remember in all business dealings is 'integrity'. Integrity is essential to developing trust: we know that a person is acting with integrity when he is not moved by opportunist or self-seeking impulses and we can trust his response to a total situation. (20.44) Integrity involves being open, honest, truthful and consistent with your beliefs in all your business dealings.

The whole of business requires trust, faith and goodwill. In the emerging digital economy, establishing trust is a critical factor for success.

Queries
: Are you honest and truthful in all you say and do? If pressure is brought upon you to lower your standard of integrity, are you prepared to resist it? (1.02.38)

Do you do what you promise, even if it is just to return a phone call?

2. Simplicity

Advice
: The most serene and happy people are often those who live a simple life. By contrast, stress, overwork and insecurity are rife in today's pressured world of

business. In business, as in our personal life, we can be consumed by our own desires for more, as well as by the demands of others. The practice of simplicity helps us to eliminate the superfluous and to put first things first. (20.35) This requires strong principles, focused vision, deep understanding, clear communication and deliberate action.

Queries

Do you make time to review your priorities in the light of your highest understanding? When faced with conflicting demands, do you look at them in the light of your priorities and endeavour to put the more important things first?

Do you scrutinise your desires and consider how you might simplify your needs? Are you easily persuaded to buy something you do not need or cannot afford? Is there a need for lavish entertainment or expensive offices? Can you achieve the same objective in a different way?

Can you simplify your processes and procedures and still accomplish your business purpose?

3. Equality

Advice

When we accept that every person has a spark of godliness within, we come to understand that everyone of us is equal in the mind of the Creator. Be alert to practices here and throughout the world which discriminate against people on the basis of who or what they are or because of their beliefs. (1.02.33)

Queries

Do you respect and encourage diversity as a source of energy in your business?

Do you refrain from making prejudiced judgements about others? (1.02.22)

When recruiting, evaluating or promoting employees, do you differentiate on the grounds of age, gender, sexual orientation, skin colour, religion, nationality or dialect, or any other characteristic that is not related to job performance?

If an employee has a disability, do you try to find work that they can do effectively? Do you make alterations in your working methods and workplace to help them? Do you help them to overcome their own difficulties?

4. Peace

Advice

Conflict happens, and will continue to happen, even in the most peaceful of worlds. (20.71) In business, as in the rest of life, how we deal with our own anger and how we find peaceful solutions to conflict are important. What matters most, however, is to work towards creating a culture of peace overcoming the potential for all war and strife. This requires searching out anything in our conduct of business which might contain the seeds of war or otherwise threaten life.

Quakers believe that there is 'that of God' in everyone. This leads to one of their most strongly held beliefs that it is wrong to kill anyone and therefore all forms of war are wrong. Conflict should be pre-empted through active peace-keeping and, when it does flare up, should be resolved while preserving respect for all concerned.

Avoid doing any business which promotes warfare in any form.

When you disagree with a colleague, customer or supplier, are you willing to consider that you may be the one who is mistaken? Do you give others the benefit of the doubt?

When you are angry, do you act in a destructive manner, or are you able to express your anger in a way that leaves room to find a solution?

What is your fundamental attitude towards business? Do you believe that success is achieved primarily by beating the competition at any cost?

Does your company earn any income from practices which threaten human life?

Conduct of Business

When we realise that everything we have comes to us as a gift from God, we understand that we are all stewards accountable for our use of time, people, money and natural resources. In each situation a good steward seeks the right balance between prudence and adventure; conservatism and creation; leading and serving; stimulating and supporting.

Good business is the way we serve the social and economic community, whether individually or corporately in national or international organisations. Its principles apply equally to commercial enterprises, to charities and to not-for-profit enterprises, because they too are managed by individuals aiming to optimise performance.

5. Business and profit

Advice
There is nothing unethical in making a profit. No business will survive for long without it. What matters is how you make your profit and what you do with it.

If you want to maintain, or even increase, employment, it will be necessary to be profitable and to build up resources for the future. Profit is also needed for new development and for contributing to the community in which you operate.

Queries
Are the purposes of your business clear to all your stakeholders? Are all its activities focused on achieving its objectives?

What is the driving force of your business? Is it just to maximise your profit or is it to provide sustainable employment for as many people as is sensible; to build your employees' confidence, skills and sense of worth; to provide a product or service that contributes to others' well-being? Does it allow for your business to be sustained into the future?

Is your profit gained in an ethical and just way? If you have little competition, do you make an excessive profit? In the conduct of your business, do you provide good quality at a fair and fixed price? Are you tempted to raise your prices and make a bigger profit just because the market will bear it?

6. Uncertainty and risk

Advice

There is an element of uncertainty and risk in every business. There can be uncertainty because we lack information about the situation, about the future or about the consequences of some course of action. There is always the risk of loss either from a particular course of action or from some untoward occurrence.

It is important to be proactive in managing and containing risks so as not to jeopardise the livelihood of your employees or the future survival of your business.

Queries

Do you regularly review the risks associated with your business and seek competent advice on how to manage them?

Do you take reasonable steps to eliminate unnecessary risks? Do you make sure that people affected by a risk know about it? Do you seek to contain and limit the consequences through appropriate insurance? Do you have contingency plans ready to deal with unexpected events?

Do you avoid excessive risks so as not to jeopardise the livelihood of your employees or the future of your business?

7. Responsibilities of directors and managers

Advice

Directors and managers have responsibilities to all stakeholders of the business. These include investors, government bodies and the community, as well as employees, customers and suppliers.

A business should fully comply with all applicable laws and regulations. If you consider a law to be at variance with your own social or ethical testimonies, seek counsel before taking action.

Seek to do away with dangers and abuses by creating an atmosphere and culture in your workplace that is conducive to health, safety, integrity and well-being as well as high productivity.

Queries

Are you aware of your legal responsibilities as a director or manager? Do you take positive steps to fulfil them?

Do you regularly review the social and moral health of your business? Do you set, communicate and work to standards of business conduct? Have you established systems for monitoring and reporting back in these areas?

If your organisation is doing something which you believe to be unethical, do you consider what part you must play to put the matter right?

Do you ensure that your shareholders receive all the information they need to rightly value and appraise their investment?

8. Obligations to shareholders and investors

Advice

Any sizeable company needs outside investors in order to take advantage of opportunities for growth. Shareholders provide necessary capital and are rewarded by dividends or capital growth.

Small shareholders have a small voice in the running of a company, but their concerns should be listened to and considered, or your reputation as a business may suffer.

Queries

Do you ensure that your shareholders receive a fair return for their investment and risk? Are you managing for the long-term security of their investment?

Do you cut corners on necessary expenditure in order to increase the return to your shareholders?

Do your communications with your shareholders give sufficient information about the progress of the company?

9. Ethical trade

Advice   Wages should reflect the contribution workers make to their companies. Wages and work requirements should enable them to meet their own needs and those of their dependants, and to contribute to the sustainable growth of their community. Very low pay could be regarded as a form of modern slavery.

Queries   Does your company invest in, or have offices in, or buy from, countries where there are on-going violations of human rights?

Does your company contract with companies which employ children under the age of 15, who are prevented from obtaining a basic education because of their work?

Does your company contract with companies which do not pay their employees a sustainable living wage in their own community?

10. Environmental responsibility

Advice   In recent decades we have more clearly learned that we have a responsibility to care for the physical and economic environment of all the world. We should no longer consider only the effect our business has on our immediate environment. In reality, the environment is a 'silent stakeholder'.

Ensure you do not cause a nuisance to neighbours by excessive noise, or the production of noxious fumes, or keeping your premises untidy.

Do you consider the way your production of goods or services contributes to a sustainable world environment? Do you have an active pollution prevention programme? Do you search for ways to reduce and eliminate waste? Do you recycle or use recyclable parts?

Do you provide a product or service which is in any way harmful to life? If so, are there clear warnings?

Do you have an environmental policy and report annually on your progress?

11. Health, safety and security

Advice   All employers and employees have a duty to ensure that their working practices and equipment are safe for all users and the general public. They should also exercise prudent security and take steps to minimise risks to the health, safety and welfare of others, whether they are employees, customers or anyone affected by the products or services supplied.

Queries   Do you take all reasonable and appropriate steps to comply with health and safety regulations? Do you compromise on safety measures to save money?

Do you work with others to ensure that best practices, standards, regulations and legislation are developed to promote public well-being?

When you see something which could be a hazard, do you report it?

12. Quality and safety of products and services

Advice

Quakers have a long-standing reputation for providing good quality at a fair price. This reputation enhanced their businesses. There is plenty of evidence to show that this is good practice for any business and pays its own dividends.

At a minimum, suppliers have a responsibility to ensure that what they offer is not likely to cause foreseeable physical or financial damage to their users.

Queries

Do you continually strive to improve the quality and safety of your products? Do you have a quality control programme?

Does your product have a built-in obsolescence, so that the customer will have to replace it soon?

Do your products and services comply with the law and other regulations? Are they safe, fit for use, suitable for their purpose, appropriately designed and sustainably produced?

Have your products been carefully assessed for any possible damage or loss they could cause to customers? Have you provided adequate warnings of any dangers? Have you ensured others can be compensated in the event that your product causes unforeseen harm or dissatisfaction?

13. Advertising and promotion

Advice   Advertising and promotional activities are a real test of our commitment to honesty and integrity in business. Consider carefully your reasons for advertising, what your advertisements say (or omit to say), and where you advertise.

Queries   Are you careful to avoid intentionally misleading those with whom you do business? Do you ensure that your claims and promises are justified and realistic?

Do your promotions present a true and accurate picture of your products and services?

Are you selling goods and services of worth or are you selling image? Are you aiming your advertisements at particularly vulnerable markets, such as children?

Is your advertising an appropriate use of resources? Are the costs of promotion a minimal proportion of the overall price?

Money Matters

Money is a complex commodity. Our use of money has the power to do great good or great evil. It should be remembered that money has extremely powerful, symbolic and psychological connotations and implications that can lead people to behave unexpectedly. In business, money should be used like any other tool – to help achieve your business objectives. More money should not become an obsessive goal in itself.

14. Investments

Advice   Think carefully how you invest any surplus funds not immediately needed. While these funds are being invested, someone else is making use of them. Is that use something you would approve of?

Seek to invest in activities or enterprises that contribute positively to the local or global economy, and which raise the quality and standard of living.

Consider the conditions under which the income is produced and the effect which the investment may have on the welfare of all. (20.56)

Queries   Does your company invest in, or earn revenue from, activities that are unethical or harmful to life? These may include alcohol, drugs, tobacco, firearms or military weapons and supplies, gambling or nuclear power.

When you have surplus funds, do you keep some back for when your business will need them?

Do you look after your reserve funds properly, or could they be used more effectively? Do you consider ethical investments, even if the return might be slightly less?

Do you use money entrusted to you with prudence, discretion and responsibility?

If you lend money, is the loan properly recorded? Do you charge a higher rate of interest than you could earn on the money if you invested it elsewhere?

15. Prompt payment

Advice Remember that payment is owed when the job is completed. Many small businesses may experience serious cash flow problems and even become bankrupt because they do not have sufficient cash to pay their own bills. Often this is because other companies – larger or with more trading clout – have not paid them on a timely basis, not because they are unprofitably managed. Make sure you pay your bills on time.

Queries Do you know and honour your suppliers' terms? Do you delay payment at the expense of your supplier?

Do you make your own terms clear and do you deal fairly and consistently with those who do not honour them?

16. Financial accounts

Advice Accounts are important statements about your business. They should accurately reflect your business position. The information they contain should be appropriately available to those who trade with you so that they can assess any risk.

Unless you keep careful accounts and review them each month it is difficult to manage the business properly. Do not rely solely on historic figures. It is important to consider the future and to try to forecast likely events.

Ensure that people handling money are properly competent, that they are honest and that they are not presented with undue temptation.

Queries

Do you ensure that you keep true and accurate accounts? Are your annual accounts produced in a timely manner?

Do you audit your accounting systems to ensure that the control mechanisms are adequate? Are you vigilant against fraud, honest mistakes and malicious deceit?

Do you provide your accounts to those who need to know about your business for their well-being, including your staff?

17. Taxes

Advice

Avoiding the payment of excess tax by organising your financial affairs so that you do not pay more tax than the law requires of you is good management. Evading tax by organising your affairs in order to escape paying taxes which are properly due is theft. It is important to consider carefully the line separating the two. Not all professional advisers are clear on the distinction.

When a way of avoiding tax is suggested, do you consider carefully whether this is avoidance and not evasion? Do you let the tax 'tail' wag the business 'dog'?

Do you deal honestly with the tax authorities? Do you consider paying tax as part of the duty of your business to society?

Do you keep careful records to prevent evasion of tax, National Insurance and VAT?

Do you keep adequate records of benefits in kind so that the Inland Revenue is not defrauded or your staff penalised?

Do you take steps to ensure that cash transactions are accurately reported for tax purposes?

18. Remuneration

Remuneration is not just about pay. It may also include bonuses, company pension contributions, privileged share purchases and services (including cars) provided by the company. It is a return for work done, responsibility and good management.

Rates of pay are subject to market forces and the current climate for high salaries for some executives reflects the international shortage of good managers. But excessive remuneration causes envy and this is dangerous to a free society.

Any differences in pay between people doing similar jobs should be logical and understood by all concerned.

If you award yourself high remuneration, does the same principle apply throughout the company? Do you have a limit of maximum remuneration compared to the minimum within the organisation?

Is your remuneration linked to profitability, even when this has been achieved by making others redundant?

Do you ensure that your wages and salaries are adequate so that employees do not need to depend on perks or other means to supplement their pay? Do you pay only the least salary and other benefits you can get away with?

Do you ensure that part-time staff receive the same benefits as full-time staff, on a proportionate scale?

Do you provide a pension for your employees? Is it fully portable (including your contributions) when the employee leaves your employment?

If your staff have to work overtime, do you give them fair recompense?

If staff live in accommodation which is tied to the job, is provision being made by either the employee or yourself for their accommodation after they retire?

Do you have a profit sharing plan, to which all (including part-time employees) belong?

19. Gifts and donations

Encourage a spirit of generosity in your company. (20.60) Set aside a portion of your profit for charitable purposes. Consider having a company day out where everyone works together for a worthy cause.

Sometimes gifts can be acceptable as a sign of appreciation, but be careful that this is not seen as a bribe. If you donate to political parties or pressure groups, be open about it in your accounts.

Do you set aside some money for charitable purposes each year? Do you give your employees the opportunity to decide how some of this should be allocated?

Do you encourage you staff to give to charities personally and do you provide procedures and mechanisms for helping them to do so?

If you give gifts, do you do so without expectation of any return favours? Are you sure that the receiver is not taking on an obligation?

If a business colleague invites you out, do you pay on at least half of the occasions?

Do you have a policy concerning the acceptance of gifts?

Working with People

Consider that in all business relations you are jointly engaged in a spiritual and practical journey. Treat other people in the way in which you would like to be treated. Remember that people have different values and that you might be dealing with people from a culture that is different from yours. Like ourselves, at different times people might be angry, hurt or distracted and they might make mistakes or do things that are hurtful.

20. Responsibility of employers to employees

Advice

Much of the Quaker thinking about, and practice of, a better way to treat people at work, which was developed during the early twentieth century, is now generally accepted as normal practice. For example, Quaker businesses took a leading part in reducing working hours, providing sick benefit, pensions, life assurance and, in some cases, even affordable housing.

One of the primary responsibilities of business today is the creation of opportunity. Employers have a responsibility to bring out the best in people and encourage their moral and intellectual growth. They should seize opportunities to improve the well-being of their employees.

If or when disputes occur, it is easier to deal with tensions and perhaps take difficult action early on than it is to try to resolve conflicts and make peace after a difficulty has become a destructive full-scale dispute. A clear disputes procedure that is known and accepted by all can take the heat out of a disagreement and allow a speedy and just resolution.

Good Business: Ethics at Work

Are people proud to work for your company? Do your employees think that your business is a good place to work?

Are your places of work safe, healthy, cheerful and congenial?

Do you treat your employees in the same way that you would like to be treated?

Do you give volunteers the same care, consideration and recognition as employees?

Are your working hours flexible enough to allow for family commitments?

Do you provide adequate training for your employees so that they can progress either in your business or another when an opportunity arises?

Do you support your staff when they decide to leave? Do you provide fair references? When you have to dismiss an employee, for whatever reason, do you do it as kindly as possible? In a case of redundancy, do you compensate your employee for (some of) the time it will take them to find another job?

Do you have a regular programme of performance reviews and do you adhere to it?

Do you seek to avoid and prevent unnecessary disputes? Do you have ways to detect disputes and deal with them before they become disruptive? Do you have a clear grievance procedure that emphasises mediation or arbitration?

21. Responsibility of employees to an employer

Advice

Your employer is providing you and possibly your family with a livelihood. You should recognise that in return you are expected to earn your keep. Whatever your position, make sure that you take your share of the responsibility to make the company a success.

The workplace provides many facilities, opportunities and distractions. For some these might include telephones, e-mail, photocopiers, internet access, and so on. Make sure these are used for the furtherance of the business. Use for private convenience, entertainment or gain should be kept to a minimum. Remember that to go beyond reasonable use is a betrayal of your employer's trust and is in fact theft.

Queries

Do you give a full day's work for your wage, salary or commission? Do you avoid wasting your employer's or client's time? Do you spend unnecessary time socialising on the job?

Do you speak up and tell your employer when there are problems or when you see difficulties ahead?

Do you ask for permission to use company facilities for your own purposes?

Do you treat your employer in the fashion in which you would wish to be treated? Do you disparage your company to others outside work?

Are you pleasant, courteous, helpful and supportive to customers, suppliers and other employees?

22. Customers

Treat your relationship with your customers with respect. Try to achieve a win-win outcome for all transactions and exchanges, where neither party walks away feeling aggrieved or mistreated.

Conventional wisdom is that the customer is always right, but this must be accepted with care. Reserve the right to decline custom from someone who does not respect your own rights.

Be careful not to pass information learned from one customer on to another where the two are in competition with one another.

All businesses will receive complaints from customers. Sometimes they are fair, and sometimes they are not; but all complaints have to be dealt with if your reputation as a fair supplier is to be maintained.

Do you treat your customers with the respect they deserve?

If you are likely to work for two customers in the same industry, do you inform both customers and tell them what steps you take to preserve the confidence of each?

If you are going to be late in delivery, do you tell your customer as soon as possible, or do you wait until he complains? Do you do all you can to minimise the problem for your customer?

Is your invoice comparable with your quotation – or are there lots of extras?

Do you decline custom from someone who does not respect your rights?

Are you willing to listen to and learn from any complaints? Do you replace faulty goods without question? Do you have a fair complaints procedure? Do you take all reasonable steps to deal with complaints as quickly as possible and to rectify an error as soon as it is found?

23. Suppliers

Advice
Treat the relationship with your suppliers in the same spirit as your customer relationships. Suppliers have just as much right to be respected as customers. They are equally important to your business success. They may also be a customer one day.

Queries
Do you treat suppliers with the respect they deserve?

If you have a strong purchasing position, do you treat your suppliers harshly? If you want to end a long-standing relationship with a supplier, do you give enough notice for them to adjust their business?

When a supplier provides credit, they are lending you their money. Do you treat that privilege with the respect it deserves?

Do you strive to achieve lasting relationships of mutual trust with your suppliers? Do you keep them waiting for appointments?

Do you ask an unnecessary number of suppliers to provide quotations? Remember that every quotation takes time to prepare. Do you expect suppliers to provide free work when giving a quotation? Do you provide someone else's quotation as a target price to beat?

Do you ask for quotations without intending to change suppliers, but only to reduce the charges of an existing supplier?

Do you ensure that you have contracts with your suppliers – for their protection as well as for yours? Do you give your suppliers prompt, clear and helpful feedback when their goods or services are not up to the standard that you ordered?

24. Competitors

Advice

Respect your competitors. Remember that together you are looking after the reputation of your whole industry. Within the spirit and intent of the law, consider working jointly with your competitors to provide a new or better product or service. Avoid wasteful or hurtful associations, cartels and monopolies that damage the economy, the environment or other people.

Queries

Do you avoid maligning your competitors?

Do you desist from industrial espionage? If confidential information concerning a competitor is made available to you, do you refrain from making use of it? Do you take reasonable and prudent precautions to protect your business and its employees from industrial espionage, hackers and malicious attacks?

Are you willing to refer a customer to a competitor when you cannot provide their needs? Do you try to entice customers away from your competitors by unethical means?

Do you avoid price-fixing arrangements?

25. Caring for oneself

Advice

Business, like other activities in life, requires that each person takes good care of themselves.

Develop personal habits, routines and rituals that limit the stress and pressure in your life. Build your own self-discipline to work and rest effectively, living a rich life of benefit to all.

Queries

Do you take sufficient rest and holidays to ensure you re-create yourself to be effective in your job?

Do you ensure that you know both yourself and your business and that you set realistic and achievable objectives? Are you learning to face issues and situations so that you avoid unnecessary fear and poor decisions? Do you seek wise counsel from both inside and outside your business when in difficulties and when contemplating new directions?

Do you know when to let go, whether it be to others, to sell, or to retire?

Are you careful to share your burdens as well as your joys? Do you allow others to take a full part in the work and responsibility of your business so that neither you nor they are over-burdened or over-stressed? Do you praise and value yourself as well as your employees?

The Community

The whole community today is an international network of people and organisations. Any business is involved in the community at many levels. First of all companies must build a thriving community within their organisation. At the next level a company is involved in the larger community which includes suppliers, customers, governments and others. At the highest level companies, regardless of size, are involved in the global economy. The world of business is one of the most obvious examples of the interdependence of the whole human race.

26. Local community

Advice

The community in which you operate consists of residents, other businesses, schools, shops and other services. Although it is easier to be recognised for what you do in a small community, in a large city the same concern for the community applies.

Try to manage your business affairs so as to be an asset to the community and not an annoyance.

If asked to support a local activity, try to find some way in which you can participate.

Queries

Are you actively involved in working for the improvement of the community in which you work?

How does your reputation stand locally?

Are you vigilant against earning undue profit at the cost of the community?

27. Government

Advice   Business is required to operate within both the spirit
          and intent of the law: local, national and
          international. Monitoring and understanding the
          impact of legislation is difficult and time consuming.
          In most instances, laws do not affect businesses that
          manage their affairs ethically; however, ignorance of
          the law is no excuse. If you discover you are operating
          outside the law, correct the situation as speedily as
          possible.

Queries   In all your business affairs, do you keep within the
          law? Do you make sure that you are regularly
          informed about regulations that apply to your
          business? Do you respect and abide by them?

          Do you join with others and take steps to change
          those laws and regulations which you believe are
          unjust or immoral?

28. Trade unions

Advice   Remember that it is the job of trade unions to assert
          the interests of their members, particularly by
          pressing for security of employment, good working
          conditions and the most favourable rates of pay
          possible. In your dealings with trade unions, work to
          cultivate a mutual trust so that both of you will do
          your best to make the organisation successful. The
          objective of negotiations is to achieve a win-win
          outcome for both parties.

Do you keep any promises you may have made to trade unions? Do you ask more from them than you would be prepared to give if you were in their position?

Do you try to avoid unnecessary conflict and confrontation? Do you consider employers and trade unions as colleagues, each of whom has a worthwhile contribution to make to the business?

29. Pressure groups

Advice Sometimes a product or service, a price, or a lack of competition might be seen by a vocal minority to be wrong. If you are affected, do not ignore the situation, but consider carefully what is said and what, if anything, you should do about it.

Queries If your business is the subject of a pressure group, do you take time to talk to them, to understand their points of view, to explain yours, and to try and come to an amicable way of resolving problems?

Do you join with others to work for a better, more moral world? Do you ensure that any pressure groups to which you may belong are morally based?

Unethical Business Practices

Many people in business have at one time or another been confronted with unethical business practices. These practices have helped to give business a bad reputation. How we respond to these situations can involve having to make difficult decisions, even to the point of blowing the whistle.

30. Gambling and speculation

Advice

In gambling we gain by the outcome of some chance event and from the losses of other people. When we invest in exceptionally risky ventures with the hope of an exorbitant return in the future, we are speculating.

Unjustified confidence and optimism or an addiction to the excitement of uncertainty can lead to disaster. In a working environment this might put your employees' livelihood at stake.

Queries

Do you invest or otherwise use company funds for speculative purposes or gambling?

Do you entertain business colleagues at casinos or other venues where gambling takes place?

31. Corrupt practices

Advice

Bribes, back-handers and other practices which we would consider corrupt are commonly accepted in some industries and cultures. Make sure that your employees know that these kinds of practices are not acceptable.

Do you have a clear written policy on business conduct which all employees sign?

Do you avoid all forms of bribery and corruption, both within your own business and in your dealings with business partners?

When you work in cultures where bribery and corruption are part of the way of life, do you try to find ways of doing business that more closely express your own ethical standards?

Do you discourage and work against sharp practice in all your workplaces? Do you speak out against the corrupt practices you discover?

32. Whistle blowing

Advice Before blowing the whistle on an organisation, or on a particular business practice, consider carefully the consequences of your actions. Your role is to be a witness to the truth. Be sure that you understand the reasons for the practice and that your evidence is clear, complete and unambiguous. Make sure that your own motives will withstand the heat of public scrutiny. Act promptly as soon as you are sure of what you intend to do. Where possible, seek advice and guidance from others. Work through an agency to remove undue emotions and personalities from the situation and to allow truth and facts to prevail.

Queries Is the action you contemplate likely to lead to a change for the better? If not, what is your motivation? Is there a better, less confrontational, way of dealing with the situation? Do you realise that your action might cost you your job and that will affect your personal life and your career? Have you sought independent, wise counsel before proceeding?

Is your company's culture one where your staff and colleagues have the confidence to deal with corruption? Do you have procedures in place so that your employees can, if necessary, blow the whistle without being penalised?

Balancing Vision with Practice

Visions, ideals, principles and aims are not enough. They need to be translated into action in our daily lives. The means are as important as the ends we seek to achieve.

None of us are perfect. Our methods and practices must take account of our own limitations and capacity for mistakes as well as the failures and frailties of others.

Balancing discipline, especially self-discipline, with freedom and exploration are perhaps the most important way that we grow spiritually and realise our business vision and goals.

33. Leadership and decision making

Advice
In each business situation someone needs to take the initiative to point the way forward and to motivate others to realise the common vision. From time to time we are all called upon to lead.

In business situations it is important to share your views with others, and consider the best way to achieve them. Consider all the stakeholders affected, not just the immediate players. Planning to realise a vision is not sufficient – it is necessary both to make a decision and to act.

Queries
Are you prepared to take responsibility for making a decision? Do you consult with those affected first? Do you avoid paralysing indecision?

Are you open to the advice and guidance of others for whom, and with whom, you work?

When a decision has been made, do you explain it to those affected, so that they understand the vision and the part which they have in its realisation? Are your decisions justified and will they withstand scrutiny?

34. Management

Advice

Good management is the skill of allocating scarce resources, planning, and organising other people in the performance of their work. This means giving people a framework in which to work and enabling them to do a good job despite the limitations.

A good manager needs to foster a spirit of teamwork in order to get the best out of his people. Determine the elements that make your workplace a happy and effective one, and then create them.

Queries

Do you respect your employees? Do you adopt an attitude of trust towards everyone, even though in some cases it may be betrayed?

Do you set a positive example to others in the way you manage your business? Does your managerial competence and behaviour earn their respect? Do you avoid destructive cultures of blame and 'put-down'?

Do you communicate your plans, concerns, and expectations clearly, appropriately and in a timely manner?

Do you delegate? Do you try to make each person's job more satisfying by giving them as much responsibility as they can manage?

If you supervise others, do you remember that this is your opportunity to help them to contribute their best? Do you give 'on the spot' feedback – both praise and correction? Are you careful to praise and reward others for their efforts and achievements? Do you pass on compliments from your customers? If someone makes a mistake do you consider how you can help the person concerned?

Do you remember that everyone has their own family and problems and may, from time to time, need your support?

When difficult situations arise, do you remember that even those who are hostile or who abuse our trust must be treated fairly and legally? Are you careful to keep an objective record of events?

35. Monitoring, awareness and audits

Advice

Every good business needs systems to monitor what is happening, so that it can be alert to problems when they emerge, and take action to correct the situation quickly. Monitoring, auditing and feed-back are important for quality control, continuous improvement and performance measurement.

These activities should take place in an open and constructive way. Those people responsible for monitoring should be appropriately qualified and respect the rights of individuals.

Queries

Does your business have sufficient systems for monitoring, auditing and assurance? Do you ensure that the people engaged in monitoring are suitable and qualified for their tasks?

Do you ensure that the results of your monitoring and performance measurement are fed back to people constructively and sensitively? Do you use monitoring and feed-back to improve people's quality of life at work as well as to improve the business's performance?

36. Confidentiality

Advice

Anything that is personal to an individual, including that person's feelings and even your observations about that person, is confidential. Treat anything in a one-to-one meeting as confidential – unless it is clearly for public consumption. Similarly, always treat discussions about an individual in confidence.

Be aware that in a business situation, under current human rights legislation, any employee might be entitled to know what has been written or even said about them in a meeting.

Comply with both the spirit and the intent of legislation designed to protect the privacy of others.

Queries

Can people confide in you with confidence? Do you use information entrusted to you with discretion and responsibility? Are you careful to avoid the use of tools and techniques that might limit the privacy of others?

Do you take care to ensure that no-one's rights, privacy or confidentiality are impaired or abused? Are you careful not to take ideas from one supplier and give them to another?

Are you careful not to use or distribute confidential information? If you receive confidential material belonging to a competitor, what do you do with it?

37. Intellectual property

Advice

Recognise that copyright initially belongs to the originator, but this might be assigned to an employer or sold to a third party. If you want to copy or use someone else's work, do not avoid paying for it and acknowledging their work. In the same way, make sure that your company's intellectual property is legally protected.

Queries

Do you take prudent steps to ensure that you do not infringe the copyrights, patents or other intellectual property rights of others? Do you acknowledge the sources of your work?

Before you make photocopies or use artwork do you check to find out who owns the copyright? Do you ask for permission to use the material? Do you make sure that the changes you make are acceptable to the owner? Are you careful about copies made for private study? Do you use computer software which you have not paid for?

Do you use all necessary legal means at your disposal to register and protect your own intellectual property?

If you or your company invents something which may, or ought to be, in the public domain, how do you decide what fee to charge for its use? Is it what the market will bear?

If you do not protect your rights, how do you prevent a less ethical supplier from usurping your copyright and charging highly for the product?

Quaker Methods for Decision Making

The Quaker method of conducting meetings for business and arriving at decisions is quite different from the way most businesses handle their decision-making processes.

First of all, our business meetings carry the expectation that God's guidance can be discerned if we are truly listening together. (3.02) The primary objective is to seek unity in decisions: to find a way forward that is acceptable to all present. This is not so easy to do, especially when the issue is a controversial one, or when there are strongly held opposing views. The outcome is not necessarily one that everyone agrees with, but one that all present can accept, in the knowledge that their views have been heard and considered. We must recognise that a minority view may continue to exist. (3.06)

There are some Quaker ways of conducting meetings which others might find useful.

The use of silence

Silence itself has no magic. It may be just sheer emptiness or absence of sound. However, the effective use of silence in business meetings can create a powerful atmosphere for the reception of inspiration and guidance. (2.16)

Quaker meetings for business always begin and end with silent worship. At the beginning the silence makes a break with what has gone before. It also gives time to focus on the task at hand and to concentrate on playing your part in discerning the way forward. Silence at the end helps to provide a peaceful closure.

Some of us have found that in tense or emotionally charged situations, a short period of silence can have a calming effect. When discussions become heated, the call for a few minutes' silence to reflect on the matter under consideration can often help.

Conduct of business meetings

Every meeting for business is chaired by an appointed clerk. The clerk's job is not just to keep the meeting going according to the agenda, or to record the proceedings in minutes that will be disseminated afterwards. The clerk's primary role is to be able to gauge the sense of the meeting, and to bring minds together so that an acceptable way forward can be agreed. When the way forward has been found, the clerk drafts a minute recording the decision, which is agreed by those present.

This method takes patience and insight, but it has advantages. It enables all opinions to be heard so that everyone should be comfortable with the outcome. It creates clarity because the minute has been agreed at the time, whilst the issues are fresh in people's minds. This reduces subsequent differences of opinion and revisions to minutes.

Meeting for clearness

This is a special form of meeting to help a person or group of people make a difficult decision or to seek guidance at times of change or difficulty. A small number of people are appointed for their special knowledge or experience to help those present become clear about possible options and ways forward. A relaxed atmosphere of trust is important and confidentiality must be maintained within the group. A facilitator should be chosen to assist in clarifying the questions. This is a time for listening with undivided attention.

Useful Contacts

Business Ethics

Centre for Business and Public
    Sector Ethics
St. Andrew's Castle
St. Andrew's Street South
Bury St. Edmunds
Suffolk IP33 3PH

Tel: 01223 357458
Fax: 01223 303598

European Bahá'i Business Forum
Wixamtree
Sand Lane
Northill
Biggleswade SG18 9AD

Tel: 01767 627626
e-mail: nsa@bahai.org.uk
Web: www.ebbf.org

Institute of Business Ethics
24 Greencoat Place
London SW1P 1BE

Tel: 020 7798 6040
e-mail: info@ibe.org.uk
Web: www.ibe.org.uk

RSA Forum for Ethics in the
    Workplace
8 John Adam Street
London WC2N 6EZ

Tel: 020 7451 6875
e-mail:
ruth.adams@rsa-uk.demon.co.uk
Web: www.rsa.org.uk

The Institute for Global Ethics
    UK Trust
17 Nottingham Street
London W1M 3RD

Tel: 020 7486 1954
e-mail: igeuk@globalethics.org
Web: www.globalethics.org

Management

Greenleaf Centre for Servant
    Leadership UK
1 All Saints Road
Sutton
Surrey SM1 3DA

Tel: 020 8408 1657
e-mail:
jnoble@greenleaf.netkonect.co.uk
Web: www.greenleaf.org

Investors in People UK
7-10 Chandos Street
London W1G 9DQ

Tel: 020 7467 1900
Fax: 020 7636 2386
Web: www.investorsinpeople.co.uk

The Industrial Society
Robert Hyde House
48 Bryanston Square
London W1H 2EA

Tel: 020 7479 2000
e-mail: sdraper@indsoc.co.uk
Web: www.indsoc.co.uk

Good Business: Ethics at Work

Religious Groups

Anglican
Ridley Hall Foundation
Ridley Hall
Cambridge CB3 9HG

Tel: 01223 741074
e-mail: rah41@cam.ac.uk
Web: www.ridley.cam.ac.uk

Jewish
Jewish Association for Business
  Ethics
PO Box 3840
The Hyde
Colindale
London NW9 6LG

Tel: 020 8200 8007
e-mail: info@jabe.org
Web: www.jabe.org.

Quaker
Friends House
173-177 Euston Road
London NW1 2BJ

Tel: 020 7663 1000
e-mail: ql@quaker.org.uk
Web: www.quaker.org.uk

Woodbrooke Quaker Study Centre
1046 Bristol Road
Birmingham B29 6LJ

Tel: 0121 472 5171
e-mail: enquiries@woodbrooke.org.uk
Web: www.woodbrooke.org.uk

Roman Catholic
Committee for the World of Work
Catholic Bishops' Conference of
  England and Wales
39 Eccleston Square
London SW1V 1BX

Tel: 020 7834 5442
Fax: 020 7630 5166

Miscellaneous

Co-Operatives
UK Co-Operative Council
1 Balloon Street
Manchester M60 4EP

Tel: 0161 829 5355
Fax: 0161 831 7352
Web: www.co-operativebank.co.uk

Investments
Ethical Investment Research Service
80-84 Bondway
London SW8 1SF

Tel: 020 7840 5700
e-mail: ethics@eiris.org
Web: www.eiris.org

Whistle blowing
Public Concern at Work
Suite 306
16 Baldwin's Gardens
London ECIN 7RJ

Tel: 020 7404 6609
e-mail: whistle@pcaw.co.uk
Web: www.pcaw.co.uk

List of Subjects

Quaker Testimonies

1. Honesty and integrity
2. Simplicity
3. Equality
4. Peace

Conduct of Business

5. Business and profit
6. Uncertainty and risk
7. Responsibilities of directors and managers
8. Obligations to shareholders and investors
9. Ethical trade
10. Environmental responsibility
11. Health, safety and security
12. Quality and safety of products and services
13. Advertising and promotion

Money Matters

14. Investments
15. Prompt payment
16. Financial accounts
17. Taxes
18. Remuneration
19. Gifts and donations

Good Business: Ethics at Work

Working with People

20. Responsibility of employers to employees
21. Responsibility of employees to an employer
22. Customers
23. Suppliers
24. Competitors
25. Caring for oneself

The Community

26. Local community
27. Government
28. Trade unions
29. Pressure groups

Unethical Business Practices

30. Gambling and speculation
31. Corrupt practices
32. Whistle blowing

Balancing Vision with Practice

33. Leadership and decision making
34. Management
35. Monitoring, awareness and audits
36. Confidentiality
37. Intellectual property

The Quakers and Business Group

The Quakers and Business Group was founded in 1998 by some Quakers who are concerned about the growing attitude of ethically minded people that it is somehow wrong to work in any organisation that strives to make a profit. This attitude is not confined to Quakers.

We recognise that business is not without its faults. This book was written to suggest ways in which we can affect the way in which business operates and can help eradicate some of those practices which give business a bad name.

Looking inward, we believe that there is much that religious organisations (including the Religious Society of Friends) and other charities can learn from the business world.

The Quakers and Business Group tries to help in both these concerns. We would welcome the support of anyone who is interested in furthering the work of the group. If you would like more information, please write to:

The Quakers and Business Group
Quaker Meeting House
58 Alexandra Grove
London NI2 8HG
UK